Reading Wo
Imaginary W

LEVEL 4

The Tree Spirit

Clare M.G. Kemp
Series Editor – Jean Conteh

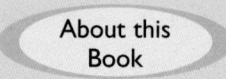

To the Teacher or Parent

This story is about a young girl who has many difficulties to overcome, including having two selfish brothers. It also teaches about the importance of taking care of the environment, especially the trees in it.

Both boys and girls will enjoy reading this book. The simple language is designed to be fun and easy for children to read on their own. The pictures will help them understand the words.

Use the book like this:

- Start by asking the children to read the book's title. Ask them to look at the picture on the cover and tell you what they think the story will be about.

- Ask the children about trees. What do we get from trees? Why are trees important to us? What would happen if there were no trees?

- Let the children read the book by themselves. When they finish, ask if they enjoyed it.

- After the children have finished reading the book, they can look on pages 31–32, where there are some questions and activities to help them understand and enjoy the story better.

Above all, let the children enjoy reading the book. This will make them interested in reading. They will want to learn to read for themselves, and so become independent readers.

'Lete, where's the water? Where's the wood? We want our tea!' shouted Mbuzi. 'Hurry up!'

Ten-year-old Lete came out of the house, carrying a bucket.

It was still dark. Nobody else was up, except Grandmother. Mbuzi and Nguruwe were still in bed. They were Lete's lazy half-brothers.

'Lete! I want some tea!' shouted Nguruwe. 'Get the water now!'

The little girl did as she was told.

Grandmother could light the fire and boil the kettle for tea, but the old lady was too weak to get water.

It was a long walk to the standpipe at the end of the village. Little Lete moved slowly. She was tired and hungry. But her brothers said she must get water and firewood before breakfast.

A year ago, life had been much better. Lete's mother and father were still alive then. Father had a charcoal business. The family worked in the forest. They cut wood and kept the charcoal fires burning. The whole family worked together, and they laughed as they worked. There was enough food for everyone.

Then, men came and built a new road. They made a big hole in the forest.

Cars and trucks travelled very fast along the road. One day, Lete's parents died in a car accident, and everything changed.

Lete's village was near the new road.

After she had fetched the water, Lete walked to the edge of the village. She looked across the valley at the new road.

The village grew bigger when the road came. People built lots of houses along the road. They needed wood for building and cooking. They cut down more and more trees. Now the forest was nearly gone.

The only tree left was the huge fig tree in the centre of the village. This was where the villagers held meetings.

After Lete's parents died, Lete and her grandmother tried to continue the charcoal business. But there were too few trees left.

Mbuzi and Nguruwe did not help with the work. The business failed.

Now there was no business, Mbuzi and Nguruwe were pleased because they had time to drink beer with their friends. But Lete and her grandmother were always hungry.

Lete worked hard to help her grandmother. Her brothers were much older, and they were strong. But they hated her, and they were lazy. They were angry when she was slow.

'Lete! Lete! Where's our tea?' Mbuzi yelled from his bed. 'What's the matter with you today?'

'I am helping Grandmother,' replied Lete. 'We need more wood for the fire.'

'Well, hurry up!' shouted Mbuzi.

'Yes, Mbuzi,' Lete answered.

Lete took the path that went past the huge fig tree. Usually, she liked walking under its beautiful branches. It made her feel happy.

Today, however, she was so tired that she tripped over its roots and landed in some mud. She began to cry.

'Somebody, help me!' she sobbed. 'I'm hungry and lonely, but I have to find firewood!'

Lete was so busy crying that she didn't hear or see what happened next.

First, there was a noise from the tree. It was very quiet, like wind in a bottle. Then there was a light in the branches. It was very soft, like cloud in moonlight.

Lete did not hear the sound, or see the light. She lay under the tree, crying softly.

The next thing that came from the tree was a smell like grilled corn. Lete smelled the grilled corn. She sat up and looked around her.

'What's that smell?' she asked.
A voice came down from the huge branches of the tree.
'I will help you,' it said.

Lete looked around. She couldn't see anybody.

'Who are you?' she said. 'Are you a stranger from the new houses?'

'No!'

The voice sounded cross.

'I am a Tree Spirit.'

Lete looked up. The light like cloud in moonlight was all around the branches. In the middle of the tree there was a kind face.

'What is a Tree Spirit?' she said.

The Tree Spirit made a noise like wind in a bottle.

'Every living thing has a spirit,' it said. 'I am the spirit of the trees. I look after the trees.'

Lete had never heard of a Tree Spirit before.

'Then why didn't you look after the trees?' she asked. 'Why was the forest chopped down? Can you bring the trees back?'

'Sometimes I hide,' the Tree Spirit said.

Then it frowned.

'I hide and I keep all the different seeds safe under my roots. Later, I will plant the seeds again.'

'Can you help me?' Lete said.
'What kind of help do you want, child?'
The kind face looked at Lete.
'I have to find firewood,' Lete replied. 'But I won't take wood from you, because you are a beautiful tree.'
The Tree Spirit rattled its branches proudly.
'Thank you! But I CAN help. Look!'
Lots of dry twigs fell to the ground.
'Thank you, Tree!' Lete laughed as she picked them all up.

The Tree Spirit watched Lete.

'You look like a young tree that is growing in bad soil,' it said, sadly.

'I've got to go,' said Lete.

She put the wood on her back and pulled the strap over her head.

'Come again,' said the tree.

Lete walked back to her house. Nguruwe and Mbuzi were sitting outside, drinking beer.

'Have you got the wood?' they shouted.
'Is it dry?'

Lete showed them the firewood. They were surprised that the wood was so good.

'Where did you get this?' they asked.

'I can't remember,' Lete lied.

'Go and drink tea,' said Mbuzi, crossly. 'But hurry! You must dig the field next!'

Lete sighed. Her brothers never let her rest.

Next morning, Lete got up very early. She was excited about the Tree Spirit. She wanted to see if it was really there. She fetched water for her brothers, then she got an extra bucket of water as a present for the fig tree.

Her brothers watched her carry the bucket down the path.

'What is the water for?' shouted Mbuzi.

Lete didn't want to tell them. But Nguruwe grabbed her arm.

'Stop! You're hurting my arm!' Lete said, and began to cry. 'It's for a magic tree. It gave me wood yesterday, so I wanted to give it a present.'

'A magic tree?'

The brothers looked at each other.

Nguruwe and Mbuzi were excited.

'The tree can give us wood, too!' said Nguruwe. 'We'll get rich.'

They pushed Lete up to the tree.

'Get the wood!' they told her.

Lete looked up at the tree sadly.

'Please help me,' she said, and she poured water over its roots. But nothing happened.

'Hurry up!' her brothers shouted angrily.
'Please help me, Tree,' Lete cried again.
There was no answer.
Her brothers were furious.
Mbuzi went to the house and got his axe and his saw.
'We can get wood from this old tree!' he said. He gave the saw to Nguruwe. The brothers began to cut into the tree trunk.

'Stop!' cried Lete.
But her selfish brothers didn't listen.
With tears in her eyes, Lete looked up at the beautiful branches. Then she saw a light like cloud in moonlight. The Tree Spirit was there! The ground began to move.

'What are you doing, Tree?' Lete whispered.
The roots of the fig tree moved aside. There was a big, black hole. The ground tipped up, and her brothers rolled towards the hole, like two rocks rolling in a riverbed.
Plop! plop! they went, as they fell down the hole. Lete stared as the roots covered them up.

'Are they all right?' said Lete.
She was worried.

'Of course,' laughed the Tree Spirit. 'You asked me to help. I have taken away the weeds, to let you grow.'

Lete picked up the axe and the saw.

'Will they come back?' she asked.

'Do you want them to come back?' asked the Tree Spirit.

Lete sighed.

'I don't want to hurt them,' she said, slowly.

The Tree Spirit looked down at Lete.

'Don't worry,' it said, kindly. 'Your brothers are greedy and lazy because they do not understand living things. If they learn their lesson, I will let them go.'

'Thank you, Tree!' said the little girl.

The Tree Spirit laughed again, and rattled its branches. Dry twigs fell to the ground.

'Here is some wood! Now go and get big and strong!' said the Tree Spirit.

Lete laughed too. She picked up the wood and went home.

Lete told Grandmother what had happened to Mbuzi and Nguruwe.

'We will stay together now, Lete,' said Grandmother. 'Let's try to look after the trees.'

So Lete and Grandmother worked hard, growing food to eat. They tried their best to look after the trees in the forest. They did not break branches from the trees. They used wood from the forest floor instead.

Lete collected seeds from the trees in the forest. She planted them in small containers. She watered them every day. When they grew, she planted the seedlings in the forest.

Other people in the village asked why she was planting the seedlings.

'We need to look after the trees,' Lete said. 'We have cut down so many trees. We need to plant some new trees.'

Some people thought this was a good idea. They planted tree seeds as well.

One day, a few years later, two strangers came to the door. They were hot and tired. Lete gave them some food.

'Thank you, Lete,' the strangers said.

'How do you know my name?' Lete asked.

'Because we are your brothers, Mbuzi and Nguruwe,' the strangers told her. 'Many years ago, the Tree Spirit punished us. We have had a hard time, but we have learnt our lesson. Now we have come back to ask for forgiveness.'

So Mbuzi and Nguruwe came back to live with Lete and Grandmother. They were not greedy and selfish now. They helped on the farm.

They looked after the trees in the forest.

1. Lete's brothers are called Mbuzi and Nguruwe. In the Kiswahili language, these names mean 'goat' and 'pig'. Why do you think Clare Kemp (the writer of the story) chose these names?

2. On pages 12–13, the Tree Spirit appears in the tree. The writer describes it in an interesting way, like this:

   > It sounds like wind in a bottle.
   >
   > It looks like cloud in the moonlight.
   >
   > It smells like grilled corn.

   These sentences are called 'similes'. Can you find them in the story? Write the sentences out.

3. Can you think of any more similes? Here are some for you to finish:

   > The sun shone like...
   >
   > The rain felt like...
   >
   > The flames in the fire looked like...

Activity page

4 On page 18, the Tree Spirit says that Lete is like 'a young tree that is growing in bad soil'. What do think this means? Write a list of the things which we need to grow strong and healthy, like a tree.

5 Trees are very important to us. Write a list of all the things that trees can give us. Try to think of at least four things.

6 What lesson did Lete and the other people in the village learn about trees? What did they do to look after the trees?

7 What can you do to look after trees? Write down three things you can do.